John Henry Newman

Prayer Book

ST PAULS

Acknowledgements

ഇറ

The publishers wish to thank the following for their kind permission to use pictures as illustrations in this book:

The Fathers of the Birmingham Oratory, for cover pictures and pictures on pp. 14, 22, 34, 38, 40, 42, 44, 50, 52, 54, 58, 59, 60, 62.

The Fathers of the Oxford Oratory, for pictures on pp. 1, 4.

The President and Fellows of Trinity College, Oxford, for pictures on pp. 6, 8, 64.

The Provost and Fellows of Oriel College, Oxford, for pictures on pp. 10, 12.

The Vicar and Churchwardens of St Mary the Virgin, Oxford, for picture on p. 20.

The Spiritual Family The Work at the College in Littlemore, and Michael Pitt-Payne, for pictures on pp. 26, 32, 46, 48.

The Parish Priest of Blessed Dominic Barberi in Littlemore, for picture on p. 30.

The Maryvale Institute, Birmingham, for picture on p. 36.

James Bradley, for pictures on pp. 42, 52, 62.

Peter Jennings, for pictures on pp. 58, 59.

This book has been made possible by a generous donation from
Sir Harold Hood's Charitable Trust

Imprimatur: ✛ Bernard Longley, Archbishop of Birmingham
Nihil Obstat: The Revd Paul Dean
5th May 2010

© ST PAULS Publishing, 2010

ISBN 978-0-85439-794-5

published by
ST PAULS Publishing, London SW11 3AS

ST PAULS is an activity of the priests and brothers
of the Society of St Paul who proclaim the Gospel
through the media of social communication.

Table of Contents

ᔐᙢᖆ

Introduction

*J*OHN HENRY NEWMAN,
writing about St Philip Neri the
founder of the Oratory, thanked God
for saints who lived to a ripe old age.
Their long experience gives us something
to draw on for every stage of our own lives.

This new collection of Newman's prayers from ST PAULS
uniquely recalls Newman's own long life in a set of beautiful
illustrations of places that were dear to him. His student days at
Trinity College, Oxford; the zeal of his teaching and writing at
Oriel College; his pastoral work in the Church of England; the
intensive prayer prior to his conversion at Littlemore; the peace
of his beloved room of nearly forty years in the Birmingham
Oratory – all are brought to mind.

While the pictures remind us of his life, the prayers make it plain
that he felt close to God at every stage of it. Through controversy,
loneliness, sickness, the parting of friends, bereavement,
Newman lived constantly in the presence of God.

The words of his prayers and devotional writings are simple and
direct. They are in some ways the best way into his heart, for
they are very often his own words for his own needs. This makes

them very powerful for us too. Whatever circumstances we are in, however long or difficult our lives, we are likely to find in the prayers of John Henry Newman an echo of the thoughts of our own hearts. In these prayers the words of his cardinal's motto really are true: 'Heart speaks to heart'.

Now that Newman is to be beatified by Pope Benedict XVI his life and his prayers are held up to us by the Church as a model for our own. More important still, we can look to him to pray for us in heaven. But beyond this exciting year we hope that it will not be too long before John Henry Newman is canonised and even declared a Doctor of the Church. To that end I would urge all those who are helped by using these prayers also to use the prayer for Newman's Canonisation printed at the end and to report any favours received to the Birmingham Oratory.

I would like to thank ST PAULS Publishing for producing this beautiful prayer book in time for the Beatification. May Newman's prayers bring many graces to all who use it.

Fr Richard Duffield Cong. Orat.
Provost of the Birmingham Oratory

Trinity College, Newman's first college in Oxford.

Prayer
ℰℭ

$\mathcal{S}$urely there are few of us, if we dwelt on the thought, but would feel it a privilege to use, as we do (for instance, in the Lord's Prayer), the very petitions which Christ spoke. He gave the prayer and used it. His Apostles used it; all the Saints ever since have used it. When we use it we seem to join company with them. Who does not think himself brought nearer to any celebrated man in history, by seeing his house, or his furniture, or his handwriting, or the very books that were his? Thus does the Lord's Prayer bring us near to Christ, and to His disciples in every age. No wonder, then, that in past times good men thought this Form of prayer so sacred, that it seemed to them impossible to say it too often, as if some especial grace went with the use of it. Nor can we use it too often; it contains in itself a sort of plea for Christ's listening to us; we cannot, so that we keep our thoughts fixed on its petitions, and use our minds as well as our lips when we repeat it. And what is true of the Lord's Prayer, is in its measure true of most of those prayers which our Church teaches us to use. It is true of the Psalms also, and of the Creeds; all of which have become sacred, from the memory of saints departed who have used them, and whom we hope one day to meet in heaven.

Forms of Private Prayer, PPS, I, 20

O my God, let me never forget that seasons of consolation are refreshments here, and nothing more; not our abiding state. They will not remain with us except in heaven. Here they are only intended to prepare us for doing and suffering. I pray Thee, O my God, to give them to me from time to time. Shed over me the sweetness of Thy Presence, lest I faint by the way; lest I find religious service wearisome, through my exceeding infirmity, and give over prayer and meditation; lest I go about my daily work in a dry spirit, or am tempted to take pleasure in it for its own sake, and not for Thee. Give me Thy Divine consolations from time to time; but let me not rest in them. Let me use them for the purpose for which Thou givest them. Let me not think it grievous, let me not be downcast, if they go. Let them carry me forward to the thought and the desire of heaven.

Amen.
MD, 384

The chapel at Trinity College, Oxford.

A Morning Prayer

ഐരു

*L*ord, I thank you that you have brought me to the beginning of this day, defend me in the same by your mighty power, and grant as I now rise after sleep, fresh and rejoicing, so my body after the sleep of death may rise spiritualised and blessed to dwell with you forever.

Keep me from the perils and dangers of this day; let me fall into no sin, neither run into any kind of danger, but let all my doings be ordered by your governance, to do always what is righteous in your sight, through Jesus Christ our Saviour.

Prayer written while Newman was an undergraduate
at Trinity, *17 November 1817*

An Evening Prayer

ഐരു

*L*ord, I thank you that you have safely brought me to the end of this day. Protect me from the perils and dangers of the night. Let me rest in peace. Let me lay myself down gratefully as if in death, knowing my spirit may this night be required of me; give me grace that whenever that time comes I may be prepared for it and that when my soul parts from this body, it may hear the grateful words "Well done, thou good and faithful servant, enter into the joy of your Lord."

April 1817

Oriel College, Oxford, Newman's college from 1822 to 1845.

I need Thee to teach me
ೲ

I need Thee to teach me day by day, according to each day's opportunities and needs. Give me, O my Lord, that purity of conscience which alone can receive Thy inspirations. My ears are dull, so that I cannot hear Thy voice. My eyes are dim, so that I cannot see Thy tokens. Thou alone canst quicken my hearing, and purge my sight, and cleanse and renew my heart. Teach me to sit at Thy feet, and to hear Thy word.

Amen.

A Daily Prayer
ೲ

O Lord, support us all the day long
until the shades lengthen and the evening comes,
and the busy world is hushed,
and the fever of life is over,
and our work is done.
Then, Lord, in thy mercy,
grant us a safe lodging,
a holy rest, and peace at the last.

Complete Thy work, O Lord,
and as Thou hast loved me from the beginning
so make me to love Thee unto the end.

Amen.

The chapel at Oriel College, Oxford.

Morning Prayer

෨෬

*A*lmighty God and Father of our Lord Jesus Christ, who day by day renews your mercies to sinful man, accept, I pray you, this morning sacrifice of praise and thanksgiving, and give me grace to offer it reverently, and in humble faith, and with a willing mind.

I praise you for my birth from kind and anxious parents; for your gifts of health and reason; for your continued care of me, for my baptism into your Holy Church, and every measure of your grace granted to me; for your gracious forgiveness of all my sins. Also I praise and magnify your name for every affliction and anxiety you have laid, or now lay upon me, and I acknowledge thankfully that hitherto all has worked for good.

Oxford 1828

Evening Prayer

෨෬

O God, give me the grace at this time duly to confess my sins before you, and truly to repent of them. Blot out of your book, gracious Lord, all my manifold acts of sin committed against you. Forgive me all my wanderings in prayer, my sins of omission, my deliberate sins against conscience.

Give me eyes to see what is right, and a heart to follow it, and strength to perform it; and grant that I may in all things press forward in the work of sanctification and ever do your will, and at length through your mercy attain to the glories of your everlasting Kingdom through Christ our Lord.

Oxford 1828

The Mission of my Life
ဆာ

God has created me to do Him some definite service; He has committed some work to me which He has not committed to another. I have my mission – I never may know it in this life, but I shall be told it in the next. I am a link in a chain, a bond of connexion between persons. He has not created me for naught. I shall do good, I shall do His work; I shall be an angel of peace, a preacher of truth in my own place, while not intending it, if I do but keep His commandments.

Therefore I will trust Him. Whatever, wherever I am, I can never be thrown away. If I am in sickness, my sickness may serve Him; in perplexity, my perplexity may serve Him; if I am in sorrow, my sorrow may serve Him. He does nothing in vain; He knows what He is about. He may take away my friends, He may throw me among strangers, He may make me feel desolate, make my spirits sink, hide the future from me – still He knows what He is about.

Hope in God – Creator, MD, 301-2

O my Lord Jesu,
Low as I am in Thy all holy sight, I am strong in Thee, strong through Thy Immaculate Mother, through Thy Saints: and thus I can do much for the Church, for the world, for all I love.

Amen.

Oriel Street, leading from Oriel College to the University church of St Mary the Virgin.

Marian Prayer of Cardinal Newman
ഇരു

O Mother of Jesus, and my Mother,
let me dwell with you, cling to you
and love you with ever-increasing love.
I promise the honour, love and trust of a child.
Give me a mother's protection,
for I need your watchful care.
You know better than any other
the thoughts and desires of the Sacred Heart.
Keep constantly before my mind the same thoughts,
the same desires,
that my heart may be filled with zeal
for the interests of the Sacred Heart of your Divine Son.
Instill in me a love of all that is noble,
that I may no longer be easily turned to selfishness.
Help me, dearest Mother,
to acquire the virtues that God wants of me:
to forget myself always, to work solely for him,
without fear of sacrifice.
I shall always rely on your help
to be what Jesus wants me to be.
I am his; I am yours, my good Mother!
Give me each day your holy and maternal blessing
until my last evening on earth,
when your Immaculate Heart
will present me to the Heart of Jesus in heaven,
there to love and bless you and your divine Son
for all eternity.

The University church of St Mary the Virgin where Newman was Vicar from 1828 to 1843.

A Prayer of Surrender

ജ്ഞ

O my Lord and Saviour, in Thy arms I am safe; keep me
and I have nothing to fear; give me up and I have nothing
to hope for. I know not what will come upon me before I
die. I know nothing about the future, but I rely upon Thee.
I pray Thee to give me what is good for me; I pray Thee to
take from me whatever may imperil my salvation; I pray
Thee not to make me rich, I pray Thee not to make me very
poor; but I leave it all to Thee, because Thou knowest and I
do not. If Thou bringest pain or sorrow on me, give me grace
to bear it well – keep me from fretfulness and selfishness.
If Thou givest me health and strength and success in this
world, keep me ever on my guard lest these great gifts carry
me away from Thee. O Thou who didst die on the Cross
for me, even for me, sinner as I am, give me to know Thee,
to believe on Thee, to love Thee, to serve Thee; ever to aim
at setting forth Thy glory; to live to and for Thee; to set a
good example to all around me; give me to die just at that
time and in that way which is most for Thy glory, and best
for my salvation.

MD, 199

O my God, Thou art in my innermost heart. Thou art the life
of my life. Every breath I breathe, every thought of my mind,
every good desire of my heart, is from the presence within
me of the unseen God. By nature and by grace Thou art in
me. I see Thee not in the material world except dimly, but I
recognise Thy voice in my own intimate consciousness. I turn
round and say Rabboni. O be ever thus with me; and if I am
tempted to leave *Thee*, do not Thou, O my God, leave *me*!

Newman's pulpit in St Mary's church.

A Prayer to the Holy Spirit, the Fount of Love

ℰℭ

*M*y God, I adore Thee, as the Third Person of the Ever-Blessed Trinity, under the name and designation of Love. Thou art that Living Love, wherewith the Father and the Son love each other. And Thou art the Author of supernatural love in our hearts – "Fons vivus, ignis, charitas." As a fire Thou didst come down from heaven on the day of Pentecost; and as a fire Thou burnest away the dross of sin and vanity in the heart and dost light up the pure flame of devotion and affection. It is Thou who unitest heaven and earth by showing to us the glory and beauty of the Divine Nature, and making us love what is in Itself so winning and transporting. I adore Thee, O uncreate and everlasting Fire, by which our souls live, by which alone they are made fit for heaven.

My most Holy Lord and Sanctifier, whatever there is of good in me is Thine. Without Thee, I should but get worse and worse as years went on, and should tend to be a devil. If I differ at all from the world, it is because Thou hast chosen me out of the world, and hast lit up the love of God in my heart. If I differ from Thy Saints, it is because I do not ask earnestly enough for Thy grace, and for enough of it, and because I do not diligently improve what Thou hast given me. Increase in me this grace of love, in spite of all my unworthiness. It is more precious than anything else in the world. I accept it in place of all the world can give me. O give it to me! It is my life.

MD, 403-404

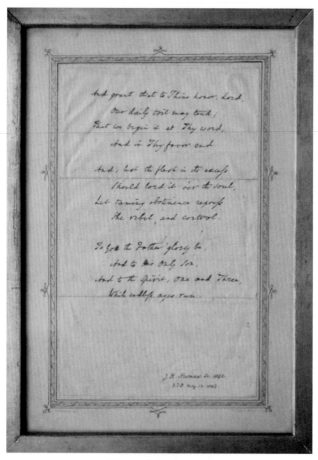

Newman's handwriting.

And grant that to Thine honour, Lord,
Our daily toil may tend;
That we begin it at Thy word,
And in Thy favour end.

Littlemore, February 1842

Lead Kindly Light
ॐ

*L*ead, Kindly Light, amid the encircling gloom,
Lead Thou me on!
The night is dark, and I am far from home,
Lead Thou me on!
Keep Thou my feet; I do not ask to see
the distant scene; one step enough for me.

I was not ever thus, nor pray'd that Thou
shouldst lead me on;
I loved to choose and see my path, but now
lead Thou me on!
I loved the garish day, and, spite of fears,
pride ruled my will: remember not past years.

So long Thy power hath blest me, sure it still
will lead me on,
o'er moor and fen, o'er crag and torrent, till
the night is gone;
and with the morn those angel faces smile
which I have loved long since, and lost awhile.

The College, Littlemore, where Newman settled between 1842 and 1846.

As speech is the organ of human society, and the means of human civilization, so is prayer the instrument of divine fellowship and divine training.

PPS, IV, 15

Prayer for Fervour
ഇᗡᏩ

*B*reathe on me, that the dead bones may live. Breathe on me with that Breath which infuses energy and kindles fervour. In asking for fervour, I ask for all that I can need, and all that Thou canst give; for it is the crown of all gifts and all virtues. It cannot really and fully be, except where all are at present. It is the beauty and the glory, as it is also the continual safeguard and purifier of them all. In asking for fervour, I am asking for effectual strength, consistency, and perseverance; I am asking for deadness to every human motive, and simplicity of intention to please Thee: I am asking for faith, hope, and charity in their most heavenly exercise. In asking for fervour I am asking to be rid of the fear of man, and the desire of his praise; I am asking for the gift of prayer, because it will be so sweet; I am asking for that loyal perception of duty, which follows on yearning affection; I am asking for sanctity, peace, and joy all at once. In asking for fervour, I am asking for the brightness of the Cherubim and the fire of the Seraphim, and the whiteness of all Saints. In asking for fervour, I am asking for that which, while it implies all gifts, is that in which I signally fail. Nothing would be a trouble to me, nothing a difficulty, had I but fervour of soul.

Lord, in asking for fervour, I am asking for Thyself, for nothing short of Thee, O my God, who hast given Thyself wholly to us. Enter my heart substantially and personally, and fill it with fervour by filling it with Thee. Thou alone canst fill the soul of man, and Thou hast promised to do so. Thou art the living Flame, and ever burnest with love of man: enter into me and set me on fire after Thy pattern and likeness.

Amen.

MD, 430-1

Newman's room in the College in Littlemore.

He who does not pray, does not claim his citizenship with heaven, but lives, though an heir of the kingdom as if he were a child of earth.

PPS, IV, 15

Continual Prayer
ഇറ

*A*s our bodily life discovers itself by its activity, so is the presence of the Holy Spirit in us discovered by a spiritual activity; and this activity is the spirit of continual prayer. Prayer is to spiritual life what the beating of the pulse and the drawing of the breath are to the life of the body. It would be as absurd to suppose that life could last when the body was cold and motionless and senseless, as to call a soul alive which does not pray. The state or habit of spiritual life exerts itself, consists, in the continual activity of prayer.

Thus the true Christian pierces through the veil of this world and sees the next. He holds intercourse with it; he addresses God, as a child might address his parent, with as clear a view of Him, and with as unmixed a confidence in Him; with deep reverence indeed, and godly fear and awe, but still with certainty and exactness: as St Paul says, "I know whom I have believed," (2 Tim 1:12) with the prospect of judgment to come to sober him, and the assurance of present grace to cheer him.

Mental Prayer, PPS, VII, 15

The parish church of St Mary and St Nicholas in Littlemore, which Newman's family helped to build through donations.

A Prayer for Unity

∞☙

*O*Lord Jesus Christ, who, when Thou wast about to suffer, didst pray for Thy disciples to the end of time that they might all be one, as Thou art in the Father, and the Father in Thee, look down in pity on the manifold divisions among those who profess Thy faith, and heal the many wounds which the pride of man and the craft of Satan have inflicted upon Thy people. Break down the walls of separation which divide one party and denomination of Christians from another. Look with compassion on the souls who have been born in one or other of these various communions which not Thou, but man hath made. Set free the prisoners from these unauthorised forms of worship, and bring them all into that one communion which thou didst set up in the beginning, the One Holy Catholic and Apostolic Church. Teach all men that the see of St. Peter, the Holy Church of Rome, is the foundation, centre, and instrument of unity. Open their hearts to the long-forgotten truth that our Holy Father, the Pope, is thy Vicar and Representative; and that in obeying Him in matters of religion, they are obeying Thee, so that as there is but one holy company in heaven above, so likewise there may be but one communion, confessing and glorifying Thy holy Name here below.

MD, 189

Blessed Dominic Barberi receiving Newman into the Catholic Church.
Bronze relief by Faith Tolkien in the Catholic church in Littlemore.

Father Dominic the Passionist is passing this way, ...
He is to come to Littlemore for the night as a guest ... He
does not know of my intentions, but I shall ask of him
admission into the One true Fold of the Redeemer.
Letter from Littlemore, 7 October 1845

*B*ut when a man comes to God to be saved, then, I say, the essence of true conversion is a surrender of himself, an unreserved, unconditional surrender; and this is a saying which most men who come to God cannot receive. They wish to be saved, but in their own way; they wish (as it were) to capitulate upon terms, to carry off their goods with them; whereas the true spirit of faith leads a man to look off from self to God, to think nothing of his own wishes, his present habits, his importance or dignity, his rights, his opinions, but to say, "I put myself into Thy hands, O Lord; make Thou me what Thou wilt; I forget myself; I divorce myself from myself; I am dead to myself; I will follow Thee."

The Testimony of Conscience, PPS, V, 17

Prayer for the Light of Truth

I should like an enquirer to say continually:

O my God, I confess that Thou canst enlighten my darkness. I confess that Thou alone canst. I wish my darkness to be enlightened. I do not know whether Thou wilt: but that Thou canst and that I wish, are sufficient reasons for me to ask, what Thou at least hast not forbidden my asking. I hereby promise that by Thy grace which I am asking, I will embrace whatever I at length feel certain is the truth, if ever I come to be certain. And by Thy grace I will guard against all self-deceit which may lead me to take what nature would have, rather than what reason approves.

MD, 288

Newman's chapel in the College, Littlemore.

A Short Visit to the Blessed Sacrament before Meditation

ဆာလ

*I*n the Name of the Father, and of the Son, and of the Holy Ghost. Amen.

I place myself in the presence of Him, in whose Incarnate Presence I am before I place myself there.

I adore Thee, O my Saviour, present here as God and man, in soul and body, in true flesh and blood.

I acknowledge and confess that I kneel before that Sacred Humanity, which was conceived in Mary's womb, and lay in Mary's bosom; which grew up to man's estate, and by the Sea of Galilee called the Twelve, wrought miracles, and spoke words of wisdom and peace; which in due season hung on the cross, lay in the tomb, rose from the dead, and now reigns in heaven.

I praise, and bless, and give myself wholly to Him, who is the true Bread of my soul, and my everlasting joy.

Amen.

Jesus Prayer

*S*hine on me, *O Ignis semper ardens et nunquam deficiens!* – "O fire ever burning and never failing" – and I shall begin, through and in Thy Light, to see Light, and to recognise Thee truly, as the Source of Light. *Mane nobiscum*; stay, sweet Jesus, stay for ever. In this decay of nature, give more grace.

Stay with me, and then I shall begin to shine as Thou shinest: so to shine as to be a light to others. The light, O Jesus, will be all from Thee. None of it will be mine. No merit to me. It will be Thou who shinest through me upon others. O let me thus praise Thee, in the way which Thou dost love best, by shining on all those around me. Give light to them as well as to me; light them with me, through me. Teach me to show forth Thy praise, Thy truth, Thy will. Make me preach Thee without preaching – not by words, but by my example and by the catching force, the sympathetic influence of what I do – by my visible resemblance to Thy saints, and the evident fulness of the love which my heart bears to Thee.

Amen.

John H Newman

God Alone
ʒℭℜ

Thomas says to Him, "My Lord and my God."

I adore Thee, O my God, with Thomas; and if I have, like him, sinned through unbelief, I adore Thee the more. I adore Thee as the One Adorable, I adore Thee as more glorious in Thy humiliation, when men despised Thee, than when Angels worshipped Thee. *Deus meus et omnia* – "My God and my all." To have Thee is to have everything I can have. O my Eternal Father, give me Thyself. I dared not have made so bold a request, it would have been presumption, unless Thou hadst encouraged me. Thou hast put it into my mouth, Thou hast clothed Thyself in my nature, Thou hast become my Brother, Thou hast died as other men die, only in far greater bitterness, that, instead of my eyeing Thee fearfully from afar, I might confidently draw near to Thee. Thou dost speak to me as Thou didst speak to Thomas, and dost beckon me to take hold of Thee. My God and my all, what could I say more than this, if I spoke to all eternity! I am full and abound and overflow, when I have Thee; but without Thee I am nothing – I wither away, I dissolve and perish. My Lord and my God, my God and my all, give me Thyself and nothing else.

MD, 354

18ᵗʰ century stained-glass window in the Sacred Heart chapel in Maryvale.

Thus the heart of every Christian ought to represent in
miniature the Catholic Church, since one Spirit makes both
the whole Church and every member of it to be His Temple.
As He makes the Church one, which, left to itself, would
separate into many parts; so He makes the soul one, in spite
of its various affections and faculties, and its contradictory
aims.

Sermons on Subjects of the Day, 10

For the Peace of Christ

ℰℛ

O most sacred, most loving heart of Jesus, Thou art concealed in the Holy Eucharist, and Thou beatest for us still. Now as then Thou sayest, "With desire I have desired." I worship Thee, then, with all my best love and awe, with my fervent affection, with my most subdued, most resolved will. O make my heart beat with Thy heart. Purify it of all that is earthly, all that is proud and sensual, all that is hard and cruel, of all perversity, of all disorder, of all deadness. So fill it with Thee, that neither the events of the day nor the circumstances of the time may have power to ruffle it; but that in Thy love and Thy fear it may have peace.

Anima Christi

ℰℛ

O Soul of Christ, be my sanctification;
Body of Christ, be my salvation;
Blood of Christ, fill all my veins;
Water of Christ's side, wash out my stains;
Passion of Christ, my comfort be;
O good Jesu, listen to me;
In Thy wounds I fain would hide;
Ne'er to be parted from Thy side;
Guard me, should the foe assail me;
Call me when my life shall fail me;
Bid me come to Thee above,
With Thy saints to sing Thy love,
World without end.

Amen.

Newman's room at the Oratory in Birmingham.

A Short Road to Perfection

It is the saying of holy men that, if we wish to be perfect, we have nothing more to do than to perform the ordinary duties of the day well. A short road to perfection – short, not because easy, but because pertinent and intelligible. There are no short ways to perfection, but there are sure ones. ...

We must bear in mind what is meant by perfection. It does not mean any extraordinary service, anything out of the way, or especially heroic – not all have the opportunity of heroic acts, of sufferings – but it means what the word perfection ordinarily means. ...

He, then, is perfect who does the work of the day perfectly, and we need not go beyond this to seek for perfection. You need not go out of the round of the day.

I insist on this because I think it will simplify our views, and fix our exertions on a definite aim. If you ask me what you are to do in order to be perfect, I say, first – Do not lie in bed beyond the due time of rising; give your first thoughts to God; make a good visit to the Blessed Sacrament; say the Angelus devoutly; eat and drink to God's glory; say the Rosary well; be recollected; keep out bad thoughts; make your evening meditation well; examine yourself daily; go to bed in good time, and you are already perfect.

27 September 1856

Marble bust of Newman by Westmacott, The Oratory, Birmingham.

Watch and Pray

ഇറ

Christ says, "Watch and pray"; herein lies our cure. To watch and to pray are surely in our power, and by these means we are certain of getting strength. ... And again, pray as well as watch. You must know that you can do nothing of yourself; your past experience has taught you this; therefore look to God for the will and the power; ask Him earnestly in His Son's name; seek His holy ordinances. Is not *this* in your power? Have you not power at least over the limbs of your body, so as to attend the means of grace constantly? Have you literally not the power to come hither; to observe the Fasts and Festivals of the Church; to come to His Holy Altar and receive the Bread of Life? Get yourself, at least, to do this; to put out the hand, to take His gracious Body and Blood; this is no arduous work; – and you say you really *wish* to gain the blessings He offers. What would you have more than a free gift, vouchsafed "without money and without price"? ... Here is your remedy.

Knowledge of God without Obedience, PPS, I, 3

And let us pray for each other, as well as for ourselves, that the gifts He has given us may not be squandered on ourselves, and used for our own gratification or our own reputation, but for His glory and for the good of His Church.

Newman the Oratorian, 221

Newman's private chapel at the Oratory in Birmingham.

An Offering of Ourself to Christ in the Eucharist

ଚ୍ଚ

*M*y Lord, I offer Thee myself in turn as a sacrifice of thanksgiving. Thou hast died for me, and I in turn make myself over to Thee. I am not my own. Thou hast bought me; I will by my own act and deed complete the purchase. My wish is to be separated from everything of this world; to cleanse myself simply from sin; to put away from me even what is innocent, if used for its own sake, and not for Thine. I put away reputation and honour, and influence, and power, for my praise and strength shall be in Thee. Enable me to carry on what I profess.

Amen.

A Holy Communion Prayer

ଚ୍ଚ

*M*y God, teach me so to live, as one who does believe the great dignity, the great sanctity of that material frame in which you have lodged me. And therefore, O my dear Saviour, do I come so often and so earnestly to be partaker of your Body and Blood, that by means of your own ineffable holiness I may be made holy. Crucify my soul and body in all that is sinful in them, and make me pure as you are pure.

Amen.

Prayers to Saint Philip

ഇരു

O my dear and holy Patron, Philip, I put myself into thy hands, and for the love of Jesus, for that love's sake, which chose thee and made thee a saint, I implore thee to pray for me, that, as He has brought thee to heaven, so in due time He may take me to heaven also.

And I ask of thee especially to gain for me a true devotion such as thou hadst to the Holy Ghost, the Third Person in the Ever-blessed Trinity; that, as He at Pentecost so miraculously filled thy heart with his grace, I too may in my measure have the gifts necessary for my salvation.

Therefore I ask thee to gain for me those His seven great gifts, to dispose and excite my heart towards faith and virtue.

Beg for me the gift of Wisdom, that I may prefer heaven to earth, and know truth from falsehood: The gift of Understanding, by which I may have imprinted upon my mind the mysteries of His Word: The gift of Counsel, that I may see my way in all perplexities: The gift of Fortitude, that with bravery and stubbornness I may battle with my foe: The gift of Knowledge, to enable me to direct all my doings with a pure intention to the glory of God: The gift of Religion, to make me devout and conscientious: And the gift of Holy Fear, to make me feel awe, reverence and sobriety amid all my spiritual blessings.

Sweetest Father, Flower of Purity, Martyr of Charity, pray for me.

O my dear and holy Patron, Philip, I put myself into thy hands, and for the love of Jesus, for that love's sake which chose and made thee a saint, I implore thee to pray for me, that, as He has brought thee to heaven, so in due time He may take me to heaven also.

And I beg of thee to gain for me a true devotion to the Holy Ghost, by means of that grace which He Himself, the Third Person of the glorious Trinity, bestows. Gain for me a portion of that overflowing devotion which thou hadst towards Him when thou wast on earth; for that, O my dear father, was one of thy special distinctions from other saints, that, though they all adored supremely and solely the Holy Ghost as their one God, yet thou, like Pope St Gregory, the Apostle of England, didst adore Him not only in the unity of the Godhead, but also as proceeding from the Father and the Son, the gift of the Most High and the Giver of life.

Gain for me, O holy Philip, such a measure of thy devotion towards Him, that, as He did deign to come into thy heart miraculously and set it on fire with love, He may reward us too with some special and corresponding gift of grace. O Philip, let us not be the cold sons of so fervent a Father. It will be a great reproach to thee, if thou dost not make us in some measure like thyself. Gain for us the grace of prayer and meditation, power to command our thoughts and keep from distractions, and the gift of conversing with God without being wearied.

Heart of fire, Light of holy joy, Victim of love, pray for me.

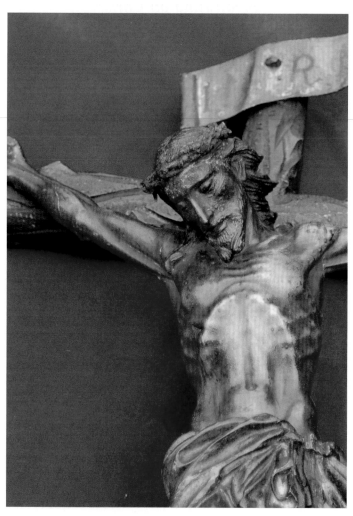

Crucifix in Newman's chapel in Littlemore.

Meditating on Christ

୫୦୯ଓ

*W*hat is meditating on Christ? It is simply this, thinking habitually and constantly of Him and of His deeds and sufferings. It is to have Him before our minds as One whom we may contemplate, worship, and address when we rise up, when we lie down, when we eat and drink, when we are at home and abroad, when we are working, or walking, or at rest, when we are alone, and again when we are in company; this is meditating. And by this, and nothing short of this, will our hearts come to feel as they ought. We have stony hearts, hearts as hard as the highways; the history of Christ makes no impression on them. And yet, if we would be saved, we must have tender, sensitive, living hearts; our hearts must be broken, must be broken up like ground, and dug, and watered, and tended, and cultivated, till they become as gardens, gardens of Eden, acceptable to our God, gardens in which the Lord God may walk and dwell; filled, not with briars and thorns, but with all sweet-smelling and useful plants, with heavenly trees and flowers. The dry and barren waste must burst forth into springs of living water. This change must take place in our hearts if we would be saved; in a word, we must have what we have not by nature, faith and love; and how is this to be effected, under God's grace, but by godly and practical meditation through the day?

Christ's Privations a Meditation for Christians, PPS, VI, 4

Newman's rosary, Littlemore.

A Short Rosary Service
℘ℂ℞

*I*n Jesus Christ is the fulness of the Godhead with all its infinite sanctity. In Mary is reflected the sanctity of Jesus, as by His grace it could be found in a creature.

Mary, as the pattern both of maidenhood and maternity, has exalted woman's state and nature, and made the Christian virgin and the Christian mother understand the sacredness of their duties in the sight of God.

Her very image is as a book in which we may read at a glance the mystery of the Incarnation, and the mercy of the

Redemption; and withal her own gracious perfections also, who was made by her Divine Son the very type of humility, gentleness, fortitude, purity, patience, love.

What Christian mother can look upon her image and not be moved to pray for gentleness, watchfulness, and obedience like Mary's? What Christian maiden can look upon her without praying for the gifts of simplicity, modesty, purity, recollection, gentleness such as hers?

Who can repeat her very name without finding in it a music which goes to the heart, and brings before him thoughts of God and Jesus Christ, and heaven above, and fills him with the desire of those graces by which heaven is gained?

Hail then, great Mother of God, Queen of Saints, Royal Lady clothed with the sun and crowned with the stars of heaven, whom all generations have called and shall call blessed. We will take our part in praising thee in our own time and place with all the redeemed of our Lord, and will exalt thee in the full assembly of the saints and glorify thee in the Heavenly Jerusalem.

MD, II

Ave Maris Stella

ℬℭ

*H*ail then, Star of the Sea, we joy in the recollection of thee. Pray for us ever at the throne of Grace; plead our cause, pray with us, present our prayers to thy Son and Lord – now and in the hour of death, Mary be thou our help.

I die in the faith of the One Holy Catholic Apostolic Church.
I trust I shall die prepared and protected by her Sacraments,
which our Lord Jesus Christ has committed to her, and in
that communion of Saints which He inaugurated when He
ascended on high, and which will have no end. I hope to
die in that Church which our Lord founded on Peter, and
which will continue till His second coming.

I commit my soul and body to the Most Holy Trinity, and
to the merits and grace of our Lord Jesus, God Incarnate, to

the intercession and compassion of our dear Mother Mary; to St Joseph; and St Philip Neri, my father, the father of an unworthy son; to St John the Evangelist; St John the Baptist; St Henry; St Athananius, and St Gregory Nazianzen; to St Chrysostom, and St Ambrose.

Also to St Peter, St Gregory I, and St Leo. Also to the great Apostle, St Paul.

Also to my tender Guardian Angel, and to all Angels, and to all Saints.

And I pray to God to bring us all together again in heaven, under the feet of the Saints. And, after the pattern of Him, who seeks so diligently for those who are astray, I would ask Him especially to have mercy on those who are external to the True Fold, and to bring them into it before they die.

J.H.N.

13 March 1864, Passion Sunday

Prayer for a Happy Death

 howsa

Oh, my Lord and Saviour, support me in that hour in the strong arms of Thy Sacraments, and by the fresh fragrance of Thy consolations. Let the absolving words be said over me, and the holy oil sign and seal me, and Thy own Body be my food, and Thy Blood my sprinkling; and let my sweet Mother, Mary, breathe on me, and my Angel whisper peace to me, and my glorious Saints ... smile upon me; that in them all, and through them all, I may receive the gift of perseverance, and die, as I desire to live, in Thy faith, in Thy Church, in Thy service, and in Thy love.

Amen.

Newman's grave, Rednal.

St Philip's Care for the Salvation of Souls

ဆ၁ၹ

*P*hilip, my holy Patron, who wast so careful for the souls of thy brethren, and especially of thy own people, when on earth, slack not thy care of them now, when thou art in heaven. Be with us, who are thy children and thy clients; and, with thy greater power with God, and with thy more intimate insight into our needs and our dangers, guide us along the path which leads to God and to thee. Be to us a good father; make our priests blameless and beyond reproach or scandal; make our children obedient, our youth prudent and chaste, our heads of families wise and gentle, our old people cheerful and fervent, and build us up, by thy powerful intercessions, in faith, hope, charity, and all virtues.

Amen.

I believe and know that all things live in Thee. Whatever there is of being, of life, of excellence, of enjoyment, of happiness, in the whole creation, is, in its substance, simply and absolutely Thine. It is by dipping into the ocean of Thy infinite perfections that all beings have whatever they have of good.

O my God, shall I one day see Thee? What sight can compare to that great sight! Shall I see the source of that grace which enlightens me, strengthens me, and consoles me? As I came from Thee, as I am made through Thee, as I live in Thee, so, O my God, may I at last return to Thee, and be with Thee for ever and ever.

Amen.

MD, 415-6

The Soul Before God
୫୦୦ଓ

*T*ake me away, and in the lowest deep
    There let me be,
And there in hope the lone night-watches keep,
    Told out for me.
There, motionless and happy in my pain,
    Lone, not forlorn –
There will I sing my sad perpetual strain,
    Until the morn.
There will I sing, and soothe my stricken breast,
    Which ne'er can cease
To throb, and pine, and languish, till possess
    Of its Sole Peace.
There will I sing my absent Lord and Love: –
    Take me away,
That sooner I may rise, and go above,
And see Him in the truth of everlasting day.

The Dream of Gerontius

*F*irmly I believe and truly
God is Three, and God is One;
And I next acknowledge duly
Manhood taken by the Son.

And I trust and hope most fully
In that Manhood crucified;
And each thought and deed unruly
Do to death, as He has died.

Simply to His grace and wholly
Light and life and strength belong,
And I love supremely, solely,
Him the holy, Him the strong

And I hold in veneration,
For the love of Him alone,
Holy Church as His creation,
And her teachings, as His own.

And I take with joy whatever
Now besets me, pain or fear,
And with a strong will I sever
All the ties which bind me here.

Adoration aye be given,
With and through the angelic host,
To the God of earth and Heaven,
Father, Son and Holy Ghost.

The Dream of Gerontius

Litany of the Resurrection
ഇൗ

Lord, have mercy. Lord, have mercy.
Christ, have mercy. Christ, have mercy.
Lord, have mercy. Lord, have mercy.
Christ, hear us. Christ, graciously hear us.
God, the Father of Heaven, have mercy on us.
God the Son, Redeemer of the world, have mercy on us.
God the Holy Ghost, have mercy on us.
Holy Trinity, One God, have mercy on us.
Jesus, Redeemer of mankind, have mercy on us.
Jesus, Conqueror of sin and Satan,   ..
Jesus, triumphant over Death,   ..
Jesus, the Holy and the Just,   ..
Jesus, the Resurrection and the Life,   ..
Jesus, the Giver of grace,   ..
Jesus, the Judge of the world,   ..
Who didst lay down Thy life for Thy sheep, have mercy on us.
Who didst rise again the third day,   ..
Who didst manifest Thyself to Thy chosen,   ..
Visiting Thy blessed Mother,   ..
Appearing to Magdalen while she wept,   ..
Sending Thy angels to the holy women,   ..
Comforting the Eleven,   ..
Saying to them, Peace,   ..
Breathing on them the Holy Ghost,   ..
Confirming the faith of Thomas,   ..
Committing Thy flock to Peter,   ..
Speaking of the Kingdom of God,   ..

We sinners, beseech Thee, hear us.

That we may walk in newness of life, we beseech Thee, hear us.

That we may advance in the knowledge of Thee, ..

That we may grow in grace, ..

That we may ever have the bread of life, ..

That we may persevere unto the end, ..

That we may have confidence before Thee at Thy coming, ..

That we may behold Thy face with joy, ..

That we may be placed at Thy right hand in the judgment, ..

That we may have our lot with the saints, ..

Lamb of God, who takest away the sins of the world,

Spare us, O Lord.

Lamb of God, who takest away the sins of the world,

Graciously hear us, O Lord.

Lamb of God, who takest away the sins of the world,

Have mercy on us.

Christ, hear us.

Christ, graciously hear us.

Lord, have mercy.

Christ, have mercy.

Lord, have mercy.

Christ is risen, Alleluia.

He is risen indeed, and hath appeared unto Simon, Alleluia.

Let us pray.

O God, who by Thy only-begotten Son hast overcome death, and opened for us the way to eternal life, vouchsafe, we beseech Thee, so to confirm us by Thy grace, that we may in all things walk after the manner of those who have been redeemed from their sins, through the same Jesus Christ our Lord.

Amen.

Bronze plaque (above) and cross (bottom right) recovered from Newman's grave in Rednal.

An Act of Love
ജയ

My Lord, I believe, and know, and feel, that Thou art the Supreme Good. And, in saying so, I mean, not only supreme Goodness and Benevolence, but that Thou art the sovereign and transcendent Beautifulness. I believe that, beautiful as is Thy creation, it is mere dust and ashes, and of no account, compared with Thee, who art the infinitely more beautiful Creator. I know well, that therefore it is that the Angels and Saints have such perfect bliss, because they see Thee. To see even the glimpse of Thy true glory, even in this world throws holy men into an ecstasy. And I feel the truth of all this, in my own degree, because Thou hast mercifully taken our nature upon Thee, and hast come to me as man. "Et vidimus gloriam ejus, gloriam quasi Unigeniti a Patre" – "and we saw His glory, the glory as it were of the only begotten of the Father." The more, O my dear Lord, I meditate on Thy words, works, actions, and sufferings in the Gospel, the more wonderfully glorious and beautiful I see Thee to be.

And therefore, O my dear Lord, since I perceive Thee to be so beautiful, I love Thee, and desire to love Thee more and more. Since Thou art the One Goodness, Beautifulness, Gloriousness, in the whole world of being, and there is nothing like Thee, but Thou art infinitely more glorious and good than even the most beautiful of creatures, therefore I love Thee with a singular love, a one, only, sovereign love. Everything, O my Lord, shall be dull and dim to me, after looking at Thee. There is nothing on earth, not even what is most naturally dear to me, that I can love in comparison of Thee. And I would lose everything whatever rather than lose Thee. For Thou, O my Lord, art my supreme and only Lord and love.

MD, 331

The reliquary containing Newman's remains, the Oratory church, Birmingham.

A Prayer for the Faithful Departed

୧୦୦ଽ

O Jesu, Lover of souls, we recommend unto Thee the souls of all those Thy servants, who have departed with the sign of faith and sleep the sleep of peace. We beseech Thee, O Lord and Saviour, that, as in Thy mercy to them Thou became man, so now Thou would hasten the time, and admit them to Thy presence above.

Let their souls rejoice in Thy light, and impute not to them their former iniquities, which they committed through the violence of passion, or the corrupt habits of their fallen nature. For, although they have sinned, yet they always firmly believed in the Father, Son, and Holy Ghost; and before they died, they reconciled themselves to Thee by true contrition and the Sacraments of Thy Church.

O Gracious Lord, we beseech Thee, remember not against them the sins of their youth and their ignorances; but according to Thy great mercy, be mindful of them in Thy heavenly glory. May the heavens be opened to them, and the Angels rejoice with them. May the Archangel St Michael conduct them to Thee. May Thy holy Angels come forth to meet them, and carry them to the city of the heavenly Jerusalem. May St Peter, to whom Thou gave the keys of the kingdom of heaven, receive them.

Come to their assistance, all ye Saints of God; gain for them deliverance from their place of punishment; meet them, all ye Angels; receive these holy souls, and present them before the Lord. Eternal rest give to them, O Lord. And may perpetual light shine on them.

May they rest in peace. *Amen.*

MD, 202

The future Newman shrine chapel at the Oratory, Birmingham.

Praise to the Holiest in the Height

&Oα

*P*raise to the Holiest in the height,
    And in the depth be praise;
    In all His words most wonderful;
    Most sure in all His ways!

O loving wisdom of our God!
    When all was sin and shame,
    A second Adam to the fight
    And to the rescue came.

O wisest love! that flesh and blood
    Which did in Adam fail,
    Should strive afresh against the foe,
    Should strive and should prevail.

And that a higher gift than grace
    Should flesh and blood refine,
    God's presence and His very Self,
    And Essence all-divine.

O generous love! that He who smote
    In man for man the foe,
    The double agony in man
    For man should undergo;

And in the garden secretly,
    And on the cross on high,
    Should teach His brethren and inspire
    To suffer and to die.

The Dream of Gerontius

Prayer for Cardinal Newman's Canonisation

ഇൗരു

Nihil Obstat:
Fr Pat McKinney
Imprimatur:
+ Bernard Longley
Archbishop of Birmingham
30 March 2010

Bronze bust of Newman as a Cardinal,
Trinity College, Oxford.

*G*od our Father,
you granted to your servant John Henry Newman wonderful gifts of nature and of grace, that he should be a spiritual light in the darkness of this world, an eloquent herald of the Gospel, and a devoted servant of the one Church of Christ.

With confidence in his heavenly intercession, we make the following petition: [here make your petition]

For his insight into the mysteries of the Kingdom, his zealous defence of the teachings of the Church, and his priestly love for each of your children, we pray that he may soon be numbered among the Saints.

We ask this through Christ our Lord.

Amen.

Anyone receiving favours through the intercession of Cardinal Newman
is asked to make them known to:
The Oratory, 141 Hagley Road, Birmingham, B16 8UE